GLIMPSES

A Collection of Poetry

Joanna Zarkadas

Riverhaven Books
www.RiverhavenBooks.com

Glimpses: A Collection of Poetry is a work of the author's creation. No portion of this material may be used without the author's permission.

Copyright© 2017 by Joanna Zarkadas

All rights reserved.

Published in the United States by Riverhaven Books, www.RiverhavenBooks.com

ISBN: 978-1-937588-74-8

Cover photo by Virginia Sands

Edited and designed by
Stephanie Lynn Blackman
Whitman, MA

On my 70th birthday
I performed my first one-woman poetry reading.
I wouldn't have had the courage to do this
without the support and encouragement
of three special women.
With much love and gratitude,
this book is dedicated to my three cheerleaders:
Ginny Sands
Judy Campbell
Lynne Wilkinson

Table of Contents

HOPE, GRACE and GRATITUDE
Heart of Gratitude 2
In the Time Before Time 3
My Prayer 4
Begin Again 5
Nighttime Sky 6
Always 7
The Ones We Have Been Waiting For 8
Born for Joy 9

I AM FROM
I Am From 12
A House of Women 14
The Intruder 15
Monkey 16
The Baker Street House 17
Visiting Yaya 18

RAISING CHILDREN
Little Buddha Baby 20
Truth 22
There Was a Time 23
Water 24
Two Blankets 25
Letting Go 26

OUTSIDE MY WINDOWS
Days Like Today 30
The Bird Feeders 31
The Morning Storm 32
An Inside Day 33
March 17 34
God Bless the Yellow Daffodils 35
The Snowstorm 36
Winter Beach Walk 37
The Salt Marsh 38
Wednesday 39
Today's Offering 40

Gifts of the Sea	41
Seaside Morning	42
Leaving Before Sunrise	43
The Twin Deer	44
The Beach Road	45

RANDOM ACTS OF WRITING

Advice on Writing Poems	48
Park Benches	49
The Wolf Under the Bed	50
At the Airport	51
The Walk	52
The Final Chord	53
52 Cliff Street	54
While You Slept	56
Past and Present	58
In My Dream	59
What Becomes of Dreams	59
Against All Odds	60

HOPE, GRACE and GRATITUDE

Heart of Gratitude

Heart of Gratitude
For warm flannel sheets on a winter's morning
For cool cotton in the midst of summer's heat

For skies decorated with stars or clouds or
Bold Crayola stripes of orange, purple, and red
For gentle ocean waves lazily lapping the sand
For wild stormy seas slamming the shore

Heart of Gratitude
For the sound of rain, the stillness of fog, the swirl of snowflakes
For blizzards that keep us inside by the fire
And dazzling rays of sun that beckon us out the door

For three shades of yellow daffodils against the stone wall
And the smell of sun drenched tomatoes
Just picked off the vine

Heart of Gratitude
For friends who sit in conversation and silence
For voices to sing with
Hands to hold
Shoulders to lean on
For those who lean on me

Heart of Gratitude
For love
For beauty
For inspiration

Heart of Gratitude
For life
With all its joys and challenges

In the Time Before Time

Before the world was even new
Before time was ever measured
Before I dressed myself in bones and skin
I knew you

I knew the sweet gentleness
Of your being
The wisdom that dwells deep in your soul
I knew the many gifts you have to share

I knew the very best of you
And you knew me
We sang each other's songs
And prayed each other's prayers

We were one
Part of the great whole
That illuminates the world
With Love

Let us pledge to each other now
That we will not forget
This time before time

But
        if by chance
                our memories lapse

Let us promise
We will remind one another
With gentle grace
The beauty of who we are
And have always been

My Prayer

I pray the prayer of the first wild winds of autumn
Scattering reds and oranges across the green grass

The prayer of fields of fresh white snow
Sparkling in the light of the after-storm sunshine

The prayer of pregnant flower buds
Bursting with new life

I pray the prayer of summer rain
Calling me to dance barefoot between the drops

The prayer of geese honking
Mourning doves cooing
Starlings arguing

The prayer of waves crashing
Thunder rumbling
Lightning crackling

I pray the prayer of tentative first steps
And frail last breaths
The prayer of cascading joys
And heart-breaking sadness

I pray the prayer of voices raised in song
And hands held in friendship
The prayer of those bearing arms
And of those bearing alms

I pray the prayer of earth and sea and sky
The prayer of all people everywhere
I pray the prayer of life
With all its contradictions

Begin Again

When this world
Becomes a distant memory
And the differences
We thought defined us
Drift away and disappear
Like clouds in dazzling sunshine

When all our walls
Gently crumble
And vanish before our eyes
When no barriers exist
To keep us apart

When we see only
The purest essence
Of who we are
Maybe then
We can begin again
In love

Nighttime Sky

After the sunset
When the red-orange sky
Turns deep blue black
Points of light
Dot the heavens
A canopy
Of a million stars
Emerges

The soothing silence
Surrounds me
The soundless music
Energizes
Each cell of my body

The trained eye
Sees organized patterns
With names and legends
I see only nature's art
And beauty

Swirling designs
Transport me
To far off places
Deep within my mind
And heart

Fill me with awe
Calm me
And offer hope
For tomorrow

Always

Even on the longest nights
When it seems
Only darkness surrounds us
And weary hearts are closed

Somewhere
A star brightens the sky
Shining its ancient light
Guiding us back
To the place
Where peace replaces pain
And love transforms our fear

Always there is hope
Always there is a star

The Ones We Have Been Waiting For

We are the wise ones
The ones who heal
The ones who know
We are the strong ones
The ones who change the world
    With a thought
    With a touch
We are the ones
    Who bring light to the darkness
    And hope to the weary
We are the ones
    Who ease pain
    And comfort fear
We are the ones
    The world has been waiting for
    The ones we have been waiting for
And finally we recognize ourselves
    As the powerful women we are
And finally we take our rightful place
    As the nurturers of our own souls,
    The answerers of our own questions
    And the creators of a world
    That feels like home to us

Born for Joy

You were born for JOY
It is your birthright
You don't need
        To search for it
        Earn it
        Pray for it
It is right here at your doorstep
Open the door wide
And let it in
        Delight in it
        Be enchanted
        Amused
        Excited
Be in awe of it
        Its radiance
        Its bliss
Wrap yourself in it
        Its pleasure
        Its wonder
Be comforted by it
        Its contentment
        Its peace
You were born for JOY
Forever and always
JOY is yours
        Welcome it
        And be grateful

I Am From

I Am From

I am from long sea voyages,
Immigration lines and bread lines
I am from old stories told over and over
And passed from generation to generation

I am from tall stern Papou in his three- piece suit
Little Yaya in her bibbed apron
And Big Yaya with her waist-length white braid
I am from spanikopita,
Chicken egg lemon soup and baklava
Salads with feta cheese, mint leaves,
And red sauce with a hint of cinnamon

I am from tealeaf readers
And violin players
Book writers, song singers, and picture painters

I am from big tin cans filled with buttons
And small tin cans filled with hard candy
I am from shoeboxes
Overflowing with black and white pictures
And dozens of photo albums
Neatly labeled with dates and captions.

I am from "Because I said so"
"We don't have the money"
And "When I was your age."

I am from cut flowers on the dining room table
Bright red geraniums on the kitchen windowsill
And philodendron plants
Overtaking the living room

I am from music in the morning, noon and night,
Homegrown melodies and store-bought CDs
I am from dancing in the living room,
In the kitchen, and in the summer rain

I am from honest apologies
And heart-felt forgiveness
I am from regrets for the past
And hope for the future

I am from yesteryears
The present moment
And a million tomorrows

A House of Women

The war created
A house filled with women
My grandmother
My mother
My aunt
Their girlfriends
And me
The Duchess
Object of all their affections

The Intruder

I met my father
When I was two
After the war released him
To home

To me
He was an intruder
An unnecessary addition
To my already perfect life

To him
I was a rival
Competing for my mother's attention
An unnecessary complication
In his well thought-out fantasy life

It stayed that way
For fifty plus years
Until finally
I opened my heart to him
Two days before he died

Monkey

My grandmother
Called me 'Monkey'
In Greek, not English
She taught me to recite poetry
In Greek, not English
She taught me to sing songs
In Greek, not English
She taught me to cheat at cards
In both languages

The Baker Street House

I remember the house
On the corner
The garden in the back
The smell of wet earth
The taste of baby cucumbers
Off the vine
I remember the long skinny porch
With chairs in a line
Facing the street
Sitting with Yaya
Waiting for neighbors to come by
With fresh gossip
To trade for strong Greek coffee

Visiting Yaya

Once a month
We made the pilgrimage
By bus, by subway, and train
From our new home
To her new home

Three tiny rooms
In the city
Smelling of incense, garlic, and goat cheese

Icons, votives, and framed holy pictures
Dominated the living room
Whispered prayers and choreographed rituals
Dominated the night

I would watch her
Through a crack in the door
From my half of her big bed
Bowing, kneeling,
Folding her hands
To her heart
To her brow
To the heavens
Not sure if I should be looking
But too mesmerized to turn away

RAISING CHILDREN

Little Buddha Baby

Little Buddha Baby
All in white
Breathing in
Breathing out

Baby T-shirt
Baby diaper
Breathing in
Breathing out

Baby round belly
Rising and falling
Breathing in
Breathing out

Baby hands
Resting on your lap
Breathing in
Breathing out

Solemn and still
Taking in the world
Breathing in
Breathing out

Cat approaches
You notice
Breathing in
Breathing out

Brother enters
You watch
Breathing in
Breathing out

So peaceful
So centered
So present

Little Buddha Baby
So dear
Breathing in
Breathing out

Truth

At fifteen
You told me
You thought
This life you were living
Was a dream
And some day
You would wake up
To see
You were sitting with God
Smiling

I told you
I believed the very same thing
You were astonished

That's the way it is
Sometimes with truth
You are so taken
With your own revelation
You think you are
The first to discover it
And it belongs
Only to you

When in reality
It is just
Sitting there
Waiting to be
Found by everyone

There Was a Time

There was a time
When I was aware
Of every breath you took
Every step you walked
Every word you spoke

I knew
Where you were going
What you were doing
Who you were with

You shared
All your dreams
Your fears
Your joys
Your hurts

I was the one
You turned to
For answers
For assurance
For comfort
For hope

Our lives
Were intertwined
Woven together
Like threads
In a tapestry

Now
The cloth is growing thin
With age and with wear
The pieces are unraveling
And with all the separate threads
You are weaving
A life of your own

Water

born of water
made of water
surrounded by water
see it, smell it, sense it
in front, behind, beside
all around me

i wade, i splash, i swim and float
and finally
submerge myself
from head to toe

buoyant blackness
covers me
carries me
rocks me

there is no fear here
only grateful relief
from a world
with colors too bright
sounds too harsh
feelings too powerful

i am not drowning
i am saving myself
blocking my ears
muting the words
i cannot bear to hear
from a child I have lost
too many times already

HIV positive
HIV positive
HIV positive
HIV positive

Two Blankets

Today there is nothing to say... except how the wind off the pond... coming in the open slider door... cools my bare feet... so that I feel the need to drape the white knitted blanket over them... even though it is summer... and some people are swimming in the sea...the blanket that came from your son... who doesn't call us or write anymore... and the daughter-in-law who used to like us... but now ignores us...the white knitted blanket that they didn't knit themselves... that drapes over the back of the blue chair...we both covet... because it sits closest to the view of the rock wall garden... and the hillside sloping to the pond...the white knitted blanket... that ties for first place in the blanket contest... with the white sheep skin blanket... that drapes over the back of the brown couch... neither of us like... because it is so deep and difficult to rise from...the white sheep skin blanket... given to us by my son... and my almost daughter-in-law... who do call... and text... and visit... and seem to like us very much...in winter you and I... sit sometimes...side by side... on the uncomfortable couch... feeling quite comfortable... and comforted... wrapped in both blankets... watching the flames in the fireplace... and talking... about the little boys we once knew.

Letting Go

I have held you in my arms
Wrapped in love
And soothed you
In wooden rocking chairs
Set in the corners
Of dimly lit rooms

I have tamed
Your wild hair
And bandaged your skinned knees

I have read you
Your favorite story
Three times in a row
For days on end

I have cheered you on
Through a million 'firsts'
From rolling over in surprise
To dates and proms and graduations

Knowing all along
There would come one day
When I would have to let you go
Set you free
To move forward
To places and experiences
I could not know or understand
All the while trusting
That our bond would never break
And that somehow
We would always be connected

One day our worlds will be reversed
It will be you who must do
The letting go
It will be your turn to set me free
To places and experiences
Neither of us knows or understands

But I promise you
I believe with all my heart
Our bond will never break
And we will always be connected

OUTSIDE MY WINDOWS

Days Like Today

When I dreamed of living by the sea
It wasn't the sunshine days
I envisioned
It was days like today
When the fog obscures
The lines between
Earth and sea and sky
When the mist blurs
The pictures outside my windows
When the long-stemmed flowers
Are bent over
With the weight of moisture
It was days like today
That invite me to stay inside
Days like today
That slow my pace
Quiet my thoughts
And beckon me
To go within
So that my inner landscape
Matches the stillness
Of the world around me

The Bird Feeders

We moved the bird feeders
To conceal them
From the condo police
Who point out page 5, section 4
Of the rules and regulations
NO BIRD FEEDERS

Now
Instead of hanging from the deck roof
In full view
They sit
On a little wooden table
Set next to the slider door
It took only a day for our feathered friends
To adjust

I sit in the blue rocker
On the other side of the glass
Only twelve inches separate us
And yet the birds seem unperturbed

The striking red male cardinal
And his dusty-rose mate
Dart about the tabletop
Feasting on seeds their friends have scattered
The ocean wind ruffles the tiny tufts
That decorate their heads
And I have a front row seat
An unexpected gift
Of this unwanted turn of events

The Morning Storm

This morning
Wind like ocean waves roared across the back hill
Sweeping up everything in its way
Every leaf and every twig, every loose blade of grass
Carried from one end of the property
To the other
Until the rock wall blocked progress
And captured all the windswept travelers

Rain frantically danced on the deck floor
Creating thunderous noise
Splattering against the windows
Distorting our vision
With its cloudy rivulets of water

Cats darted from room to room
Window to window
Both terrorized and energized
By the sound and movement

This afternoon
Light blue sky sits above us
Pale yellow sun offers its light
Freshly washed green grasses glisten brightly
Newly bared trees show off
Their stark graceful branches

All is quiet and serene
Both cats find a spot of warm sunshine on the rug
For their naps
And I contemplate nature's reminder
Every storm
No matter how tumultuous
Must come to an end

An Inside Day

Today is an inside day
Sills are soaked
With wind-blown rain
Windows are streaked
With streams of water
Not a speck of blue in the sky
The steel grey sea
Ripples with foamy white waves
Rolling one after the other
To shore

Today is an inside day
A day for reading a favorite book
Watching old movies
And playing board games with friends
A day for grilled cheese sandwiches
And tomato soup
Served in thick handled mugs
A day for remembering
And sharing long-forgotten stories
Of childhood adventures

Today is an inside day
A day with endless time for daydreaming
Or listening to the alternating rhythms
Of falling rain
And the sweeping sounds
Of wind through trees

Today is an inside day
A day for noticing the quiet messages
Of my own heart

March 17

Tiny crocuses have poked through the ground
Crayola-colored flowers are getting ready to bloom
All trace of snow has disappeared
The ice skim is off the pond
The light lingers longer
The air smells different
...Feels different
Change is happening
Earth is readying herself
For Spring's grand entrance

God Bless the Yellow Daffodils

God bless the yellow daffodils
That line the rock walls
And white picket fences
They made it through
The spring snow
To stand up tall once again
Tilting their bright faces
Shyly
Unaware of their graceful beauty
They always make me smile

The Snowstorm

The snowstorm has transformed the world
The sand pits
Are an alien landscape
Beautifully rounded mounds of white
Amid sharply pointed mountain tops
The deck furniture
Stacked and secured
Against the railings
A modern day sculpture
Of lines and angles
Tiny bird prints on the stark white ground
Avian hieroglyphics

Swirling snow stings the skin
Darkened sky blocks the sun
The world stands still
Immobilized
Waiting
I am stilled as well
My heart frozen
With indecision

As the wind sifts through the snow drifts
Rearranging the scenery
I wait
For truth to sift through my heart
Rearranging all my doubts and fears
My distorted images
Of yesterday, today and tomorrow

I long to see clearly
All the parts of my world

Winter Beach Walk

Along the empty beach
Low tide
Makes the waves lazy and quiet
Leaving the shoreline
Solid and smooth
The wind
Gentle and soft

I follow the path
Of those who went before me
Admiring the unplanned work of art
Their footprints created in the sand

My treasures
A perfect white rock
To hold in my right hand
One lumpy grey streaked rock
For my left
Both reminders of how life can be
And a single piece of sea glass
For my pocket

The Salt Marsh

My eyes are drawn
To the waving grasses
Not green
But tan
The color of straw
Long thin stems with lacy tops
Swaying back and forth
In the gentle wind

They frame the saltmarsh
Where the water is still and quiet
An almost low tide
Beginning to uncover
The dark brown mud flats
Just beneath the surface

At the end of the day
The water will be high
And deep
Nothing of what is below
Will be visible

How like the saltmarsh
Are we
Who keep parts of our selves
Safely hidden from view

Wednesday

A bank of clouds met the sea on the horizon
Looking like mountains along the shore

Blue-green stripes painted the water
The colors blending into each other like a Monet painting

The low tide waves lapped so gently on the shore
They made barely a sound

The beach stretched smooth and clear
Cleaned of all seaweed and rocks

I sat watching the shadow of my windblown hair in the sand
While holding a perfect white stone in each of my hands

Today's Offering

My offering today
Is a gentle grey morning
Of muted colors

An afternoon of quiet rain
Dancing on the walkways
A thousand ripples
On the pond
Overlapping and expanding
To the water's edge

I offer you
The distant cry of a lone bird
Longing for its mate
And the softest rumble of thunder
That soothes like a lullaby

I gift you
The one hundred
Jeweled water drops
Caught in the tiny sections
Of my screen door
The last yellow rose
Still in full bloom by the rock wall
And three red tomatoes
Bathed in rain drops

This is my offering today
An ordinary October morning
Of unassuming beauty

May it be a blessing

Gifts of the Sea

Some nights
The thick salt air
Fills my bedroom
Quietly entering
Through the open window

I breathe in the dampness
And feel the extra weight
Of my quilt
Laden with moisture
While far off
A warning bell tolls
For the sailing ships
Lulling me to sleep

It is always
A welcome surprise
This tangible reminder
That I live by the sea

Some mornings
The air is so dense
With fog
That ocean and sky
Blend into one
No horizon can be seen

The beach walkers
Are shadow people
Revealing themselves
For only that one moment
They are passing by my side

Invisible birds
Call to each other
Unseen waves lap the shore
And I am a cloud traveler
Alone in space
Relaxing into my solitude

Seaside Morning

A silent seaside morning
Fog softens the world
Muting colors, shapes, and sounds

No barrier between sea and sky
No distinction between you and me
We are one

"A quiet morning,"
        Says a voice from the grayness
"Beautiful," I whisper
"Just a different style,"
        He answers
As he picks almost invisible tomatoes
From vines as tall as he

His words remind me
No judgment
All is neutral
Everything is as it should be
Always

Leaving Before Sunrise

Leaving before sunrise
The crickets are still singing
My car glistens with last night's dew

Sea and sky are the same
Nondescript grey
The horizon line is invisible

No dogs are barking or walking
No runners are running
Traffic lights change only for me

The stillness allows me
To hear all my thoughts
Ask all my questions
And sometimes find the answers

The Twin Deer

The twin deer visited yesterday
At dusk
I watched through the window
As they strolled through the gardens
Checking the raspberry plants
The newly planted marigolds
The yellow rosebush

When they caught me looking
One sauntered up the hill
The other stood her ground
Staring at me
With her round dark eyes

For five minutes
We gazed in silence
Then she cocked her head a bit
As if waiting for me to speak
I mimicked her
Neither of us uttered a word

Maybe next time
We will know what to say
To each other

The Beach Road

This morning
Before the sun
Breathed in the moist ocean air
Before the sky
Changed her grays to blues
Before the joggers jogged
And the dog walkers walked
Before the tiny cottage windows
Were lit with light
A lone deer and I
Traveled the quiet beach road
Together
Each of us in our own lane

With her long lean legs
She matched her pace with mine
With my four round wheels
I matched my pace with hers
We gazed at each other
With curiosity
Until she turned left
Through the grasses towards the pond
And I continued my long journey north
For a playdate with my granddaughter
Maybe next Wednesday
We will meet again

RANDOM ACTS OF WRITING

Advice on Writing Poems

He tells me there are poems that beg to be written
They cling to us like burrs from the forest trail
Hang on to our pant legs

No matter how hard we try to pull them off
Some small piece always remains
Embedded in the cloth

We are not always aware of its presence
Unitl we move a certain way and feel
Its sudden piercing of our tender skin

It's best, he says,
To pay attention
To its clamoring for recognition
And write it down before
It burrows so deep
It becomes painful to extract

Park Benches

Empty park benches
Call to me
How would it be
To simply
Sit
Forever
Unmoving
Watching a world go by

Summer sun
Would warm my shoulders
And tan my bare skin

Fall leaves
Would dance around my feet
Gather in little piles
Then fly away
On the wind

Winter snows
Would blanket me
Turn me into a frozen sculpture
Startling passers-by

Spring rain
Would soak my hair
Plaster clothes to skin
Create puddle mirrors

Without leaving my seat
I could gaze into my own eyes
To find the answers
To all the questions of a lifetime

The Wolf Under the Bed

The wolf who lives here
Doesn't bite
Mostly he stays hidden
Way under the bed

On nights my foot escapes the covers
For a bit of air
He sometimes nibbles my toes

On nights my arm drapes over the side
Dangling down towards the floor
He nuzzles my fingers
But never does he bite

All my life he's been with me
Moving from house to house
Bed to bed

He never shows himself
And I have never
Even as a child
Invaded his privacy
By peeking under the bed skirt

We are friends
He and I
I trust him to treat me gently
He trusts me
Not to be swayed
By anti-wolf propaganda

We get along just fine

At the Airport

Tall and lanky
All arms and legs
Head bent to the ground
Eyes darting left and right
Watchful, vigilant

Twelve years old
Terrified
Wearing his too small Superman costume
Flanked by his family

A mother and big brother on one side
A father and two little sisters on the other
His protectors against the noise and chaos
Of one hundred travelers rushing by

My heart went out to him
My praise went out to his parents
Allowing him to wear the one thing
That would give him the courage to fly

The Walk

Somewhere
On Prince Edward Island
Off the coast of Canada
Behind an old farmhouse
Turned into a bed-and-breakfast
Is a steep green hill
Dotted with wildflowers
Where my brother Charlie and I
Took our first ever
Almost adult
Walk together
Had our first ever
Almost adult
Conversation together
About our
Almost adult parents
Both of us acknowledging
How rare an occurrence
This was
How much we enjoyed it
How committed we were
To doing it again
I wonder if he remembers

The Final Chord

The song began many years ago
A wisp of a melody
Carried by wind and ocean
Across decades
Through lifetimes
So much a part of us
We didn't realize we were singing

Now the simple grows complex
New themes
Different harmonies
Descants
Key changes
Imprints of who we are
A brand-new piece emerging

Major chords turned to minor
Harmonious triads to dissonant
Melodious sounds to haunting

The song feels incomplete
The final notes still unresolved
Who will add the final chord

52 Cliff Street

This house is alive
With color, shape, texture, and sound
Every surface holds a trinket
Every window pane an artist's display

> Hanging treasures
> Nesting treasures
> Bundled treasures

Baskets, boxes, piles
Fresh flowers and potted plants
Wind chimes and light catchers

> Sea glass
> Shells
> Beach rocks

Drawings, photographs, and cards
Books, books, and more books
And music everywhere

Sheet music scattered on the floor
Piano tunes drifting out the open windows
Voices in joyful harmony filling the rooms

This house has a pulse
It lives and breathes
There is nothing static here
Its heart beats steadily

    Spirited
    Vibrant
    Radiant

This house is throbbing with life
This house sings with joy
Each room is filled
With Creativity and Love

    This house reflects
    The hearts and souls
    Of those who call it home

While You Slept

I was with you last night while you slept
Though you never knew
And never could have imagined
How I might have traveled
So far
In the middle of the night
From my house to yours

I was with you last night while you slept
Peacefully on your stomach
Facing right
Arms to either side
Bent at the elbows
Like a babe in slumber

You were wearing
Your silk cream-colored nightshirt
That now hangs on its hook
On the back of your bedroom door
Your eyes without mascara
So relaxed
Your face wiped clean of make-up
So smooth

I was with you last night as you slept
But never once
Did I move
Or make a sound
That might have startled you awake

Instead I watched you sleep
From that crowded space
Between the bed
And the windowed wall of books
Wondering
What images caused your eyelids
To flutter every now and again
And what sweet adventures
Your dreams
Were bringing you

I was with you last night while you slept
And you never knew
Because I flew through the black night
With invisible wings that make no sound
And I landed as softly as feathers on snow

I was with you last night while you slept
And even I don't understand
How this magic happened

Three Poems on Dreams

Past and Present

When I was a child
I dreamed of under-bed monsters lurking
And guardian angels hovering
I dreamed of laundry baskets
Filled to overflowing
With spinach that had to be eaten
And thick clots of blood flowing unstoppable from my body
I dreamed of fires leaving me homeless
And death leaving me motherless
I dreamed of falling, falling, falling
And startled myself awake
Just before the landing
I dreamed of joyful leaping steps
That propelled me twenty feet at a time
And I dreamed of flying, flying, flying

Today I dream
Of grown men as little boys
Of dead parents as young and vital
Of old loves as withering bouquets
Of new loves as soft whispers

I never fall anymore
And though my body has forgotten
The child-like power of flight
There are still times
When my spirit soars

In My Dream

In my dream
My wide flowing white cotton pants
Billow in the wind
The tiny silver sequins
On my angel-sleeved blouse
Sparkle in the streaming sunlight

I teeter at the highest peak of the mountain
Or the very edge of the eave on the sloping roof
Or the middle of the wide gaping door of the plane
Almost ready
A breath away
From letting go
From taking the final step
Wondering
If I am heading towards
A disastrous free-fall
Or if the graceful currents of the wind
Will support me
As I effortlessly fly

What Becomes of Dreams

Some of them turn into amusing anecdotes
That make you laugh out loud
Some become ghosts that haunt me
Some raise questions that are hard to answer
Some become catalysts for great works
Some I try to forget
And some I struggle to remember

Against All Odds

Against all odds
The crocus blooms
Through the snow

The sun breaks through
The cloud filled sky

Grace greets us
In the midst of despair

We rise again
After crumbling to the ground

Joy blossoms
In unlikely places

Against all odds
I realize that what I want
Is what I have
And I give thanks

www.ingramcontent.com/pod-product-compliance
Lightning Source LLC
Chambersburg PA
CBHW060427050426
42449CB00009B/2168